Dennis the Menace

Dennis has come a long way since he first burst into newsprint, his hair in his eyes and a trail of jam behind him.

Here in DENNIS THE MENACE RIDES AGAIN is the little guy at his irrepressible best—a professional tyrant, a sophisticate in short pants, an old hand at puncturing large egos, a remorseless operator with a streak of bravura a mile wide. And as much as we (and millions of others) love him for his high-jinks and high spirits, we love him even more for doing—with incredible aplomb —the things we never dare to do ourselves.

Other Fawcett Crest Books
by Hank Ketcham:

Available Wherever Paperbacks Are Sold

Dennis the Menace
Rides Again

by Hank Ketcham

A FAWCETT CREST BOOK

FAWCETT PUBLICATIONS, INC., *Greenwich, Conn.*

MEMBER OF AMERICAN BOOK PUBLISHERS COUNCIL, INC.

● ● ● ● ● ● ●

Published by Fawcett World Library,
67 West 44th Street, New York, N. Y. 10036.
Printed in the United States of America

"*SURE* I'M SURE MY MOTHER'S NOT HOME!"

"IT'S ALL RIGHT, DAD. I DIDN'T USE YOUR TOBACCO. I PUT COCOA IN IT!"

"I'VE GOT THE STRAINER AND THE BIG KETTLE. AS SOON AS YOU
FIND THE FRYING PAN I CAN START DINNER."

"YEAH, I HEARD YOU SAY 'COME ON, CHILDREN.' DIDN'T YOU HEAR ME SAY 'DON'T *BOTHER ME*'?"

"HE *TOLD* YOU WHY. HE WAS AFRAID IT WOULD GET IN YOUR SOUP."

"DO IT AGAIN, DAD!"

"WAKE UP, DAD!"

"AM I GONNA PICK UP MY TOYS? YOU MEAN I HAVE A CHOICE?"

"YES, I CAN SEE THE BALL. ANYMORE QUESTIONS?"

"WELL? *NOW* ARE YOU READY TO SAY YOU'RE SORRY?"

"GEE, YOU'RE *LOTS* OF FUN! ARE YOU *SURE* YOU'RE A GIRL?"

"I THOUGHT I'D COME AND MEET YOU, DAD, SO I COULD TELL YOU *MY* SIDE OF THE STORY."

"IT'S NOT A REAL TATTOO, ALICE. IT COMES OFF WITH SOAP AND WATER."

"DEAR, WILL YOU LOOK AND SEE IF THERE ARE A COUPLE OF FROGS IN YOUR BRIEFCASE?"

"DON'T YOU REMEMBER? MOM SAID OPEN ALL THE WINDOWS
IF HE LIGHTS ONE OF THOSE CHEAP CIGARS."

"I'LL BET YOU'LL BE GLAD TO GET HOME AND PUT ON YOUR OLD CLOTHES, TOO!"

"IT'S JUST A CATERPILLAR, BUT DON'T TELL NOBODY."

"HEY, MOM! MRS. GERBER'S CARDS ALL LOOK LIKE LITTLE *VALENTINES!*"

"THESE ARE THE PARKER KIDS, MOM. THEIR BATHTUB ISN'T WORKING."

"GEE, YOU ACT LIKE YOU NEVER *FELT* AN ICICLE BEFORE."

"WHY DO YOU CALL IT *MY* BEDROOM IF I CAN'T
EVEN LOCK THE DOOR?"

"I'M JUST A LITTLE KID. I'LL GET _SICK_ IF I DON'T EAT ANY LUNCH!"

"I FELT SORRY FOR YOU. YOU LOOKED SO HOT."

"DON'T YOU PEOPLE EVER SLEEP?"

"ME 'N PHILIP WAS PLAYIN' MECHANIC UNDER THE CAR.
AND GUESS WHAT.... WE STRUCK *OIL!*"

"FAMILY NAMED MITCHELL LIVE NEXT DOOR ON THAT SIDE.
MAN AND WIFE AND A LITTLE ...... OH, BROTHER!"

"BUT I DON'T *WANT* TO WASH MY HAIR!"

"WHAT YOU NEED IS SOME NEW *SOCKS!*"

"HE WANTED IT FOR HIS *WATER PISTOL!*"

"THE GAME'S HELD UP FOR A FEW MINUTES. SOME KID RAN OFF WITH......*WHERE'S DENNIS?*"

"WAIT 'TIL SHE OPENS *MY* PRESENT. SHE DIDN'T BELIEVE ME WHEN I TOLD HER IT WAS NOTHIN'."

"I LOST MY APPETITE IN MRS. WILSON'S KITCHEN."

"WHAT A SWELL PARTY! MRS. TAYLOR DROPPED THE CAKE AND MOST OF THE GIRLS WOULDN'T EAT ANY!"

"I THINK I'LL TURN ON THE TELEVISION. OKAY? HUH? OKAY IF I TURN IT ON? DAD? MOM? OKAY?...."

"DON'T WORRY. HE'LL MAKE A LOT OF NOISE, BUT HE'S TOO OLD TO CLIMB UP HERE."

"*MY* SPOON ISN'T GREASY!"

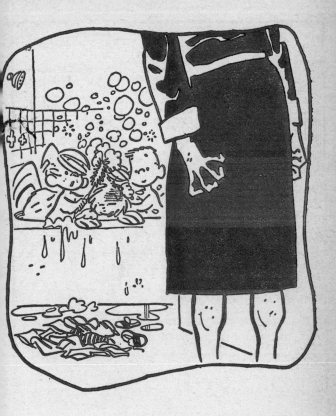

"OH, WAS THIS *YOUR* WATER, DAD?"

"WHAT'S AFTER YOU *THIS* TIME?"

"AW, JUST THIS ONCE! IT'S HIS *BIRTHDAY!*"

"WHAT'S THE MATTER? I *ALWAYS* GREASE MY WHEELS WITH PEANUT BUTTER!"

"Pssst! When're they gonna ask me if I'm thirsty?"

"DENNIS! COME OUT OF THERE!"

"THE PAINTERS WERE HERE, BUT THEY GAVE UP AFTER ABOUT A HALF-HOUR."

"COULD YOU HEAR MY DAD SNORING UP WHERE YOU WERE?"

"IT'S NOT A *REAL* ARROW, SWEETHEART! IT'S JUST A GAG ARROW THAT I BOUGHT IN A NOVELTY SHOP. ALICE? HONEY!"

"BOY, WHAT A BIG, FAT FLY *HE* WAS!"

"THAT WAS JUST FOR LAUGHS, DAD. I'LL TURN IT ON SLOW THIS TIME."

"AND I CAN'T FIND MY MOTHER, EITHER!"

"SEE? ONCE THEY'RE DEAD,
THEY'RE *DEAD!*"

"BUT BIRDS DON'T *LIKE* SOAPY BATH WATER!"

"YES, YOU REALLY SCARED ME NOW, **GET BACK INTO BED!**"

"DON'T EVER LET ANYONE TELL YOU A BED SHEET IS GOOD AS A REAL PARACHUTE!"

"... KNIFE, DOG BISCUIT, YO-YO, RABBIT FOOT... *GEE*, DAD, I *KNOW* I HAD A PIECE OF CANDY FOR YA HERE SOMEPLACE!"

"I DIDN'T TAKE ANY CHOCOLATE OUT OF THE CUPBOARD! THIS IS *MUD!*"

"FUNNY LETTER, CROOKED LETTER, ROUND
LETTER, STRAIGHT LETTER...."

"SPANK HIM? I SHOULD SAY *NOT!*"

"PUT YOUR DOG ON. RUFF WANTS TO BARK AT HIM."

"OKAY IF I LOOK AT YOUR FUNNY PAPER, MISTER?"

"WAIT 'TIL YOU SEE HOW NEAT WE'VE BEEN STACKING THE DIRTY DISHES, MOM!"

"YOU WERE RIGHT, MOM. I'M TOO LITTLE TO USE GLUE."

"YOU *FOUND* HIM, DAD! GOOD FOR YOU!
I THOUGHT THAT FROG WAS LOST!"

"LOOK! I *TOLD* YOU HE DOESN'T KNOW WHAT HE'S EATING FOR BREAKFAST."

"YOUR MOTHER CATCH YOU SWIPIN' COOKIES?"

"HEY, YOU WANNA SEE A GOOD DOG MOVIE?"

"DID YOU NOTICE I WENT RIGHT ACROSS THE KITCHEN WITHOUT GOING NEAR THE COOKIE JAR?"

"TELL ME... WAS IT DENNIS WHO YELLED 'HAPPY BIRTHDAY' WHEN WE LIT THE CANDLES?"

"I DON'T WANNA GO ANYWHERE I CAN'T RIDE A HORSE!"

"... AND YOU'RE GOING TO *STAY* IN THERE UNTIL YOU CHANGE YOUR ATTITUDE, YOUNG MAN! DO YOU HEAR ME?"

"CAN RUFF INVITE A FRIEND FOR SUPPER?"

"AND IF YOU HURT HER AGAIN, I'LL *KICK* YOU AGAIN!"

"YOU LOOK HUNGRY. WHY DON'T YOU ASK YOUR MOM FOR TWO PEANUT BUTTER SANDWICHES?"

" MY FOLKS ARE GETTING TO THE AGE NOW WHERE
THEY EXPECT ME TO HANG MY CLOTHES UP. "

" Pssst.... MAKE HIM DESCRIBE ME AGAIN."

"YOU SURE DON'T SOUND LIKE GOLDILOCKS TO ME!"

"YES, HE'S HERE. HE SAID HE CAME OVER TO GIVE YOU A REST."

"YOU SHOULDA HEARD THE AWFUL NAMES MR. WILSON CALLED ME THROUGH THE HOLE IN HIS WINDOW!"

"BOY! WHAT KIND OF WOOD IS MY BED *MADE* OF?"

"WANT TO FINISH PAINTING THE BASEMENT FLOOR?
A CAN FELL DOWN AND STARTED IT."

* WHY *AIN'T* HE SEE IT? IT'S A DOG MOVIE, ISN'T IT? HE'S A *DOG*, ISN'T HE? *

"WILL YOU PLEASE PIPE DOWN? I DON'T *WANT* YOU
TO HOLD MY GLASSES!"

"I ALREADY TRIED TO HELP MOM, BUT SHE
SENT ME OUT TO HELP YOU."

"YOU WERE RIGHT, MOM! HER BEDS AREN'T MADE!"

"IT DIDN'T COST ME *ANYTHING!* I JUST TRADED MY TRICYCLE FOR IT."

"DON'T YOU REMEMBER? I TOLD YOU I
WAS HAVING GUESTS FOR BREAKFAST."

"TELL ME WHEN HE'S EATEN A NICKEL'S WORTH."

"MR. RAGAN! WOULD YOU MOVE ME OUT OF HIS REACH?"

" WHAT DO YOU MEAN 'DIRTY OL' BOTTLES'? I CAN GET
TWO PENNIES EACH FOR MOST OF 'EM!"

"THAT'S BATHROOM WATER..... I WANTED *KITCHEN* WATER!"

"THINK, MARTHA, *THINK!* IF WE DON'T FIND A BABY SITTER FOR THE MITCHELLS, THEY'LL BRING HIM OVER HERE!"

"I'M JUST GARGLING. WHO SAID I WAS DROWNING IN THE BATHTUB?"

"WHY DIDN'T YOU COME OUT? YOU NEVER **SAW** SO MANY PLANES!"

"WOULD IT HURT ANYTHING IF I LEFT THE WATER RUNNING
IN THE BATHROOM?"

"I *KNOW* IT'S YOUR GOOD CAMERA, DAD! I WANT THIS TO BE A GOOD PICTURE!"

"VERY WELL, SIR. IF YOU DON'T WANT TO BUY A VACUUM CLEANER, YOU DON'T HAVE TO BUY ONE. *NOW OPEN THAT DOOR, DENNIS!*"

"YOU SURE HAVE A DIRTY FRONT YARD!"

I SAID, IF YOU WANT MY BUSINESS, YOU'RE GONNA HAVE TO PUT IN LOWER WINDOWS!

"YOU MEAN THE ICE CREAM IS *GONE?* DO YOU S'POSE IT *MELTED,* OR *SOMETHIN'?*"

"*I* SAY IT'S ALL YOU CAN DRINK. *THAT'S* WHO SAYS IT'S ALL YOU CAN DRINK!"

"FOR GOSH SAKES! WHAT'S CUTE ABOUT TAKIN' A BATH?"

"I *TOLD* YOU WHY! I'M GONNA WATCH A COWBOY MOVIE AT NINE O'CLOCK, AND MY FOLKS SEND ME TO BED AT EIGHT."

"LISTEN, ALICE, HE'S JUST FAKING BECAUSE HE KNOWS
YOU'LL JUMP ON ME! ALICE, LISTEN A MINUTE . . ."

"WE COULD GO DOWN TO THE CANDY STORE IF YOU'D ASK
YOUR PRETTY MOTHER FOR A DIME."

"NOW DON'T FRIGHTEN IT!"

"HEY, DAD! I'M ALL OUT OF PAPER CUPS!"

"BETCHA DON'T KNOW WHAT I'M GONNA DO!"

"LOCK THE DOOR! HIS FOLKS MAY TRY AN' GET HIM BACK!"

"YOU'D THINK THERE WASN'T ANOTHER DRUM IN TOWN! HALF
THE PEOPLE ON THIS STREET WANT TO BUY *MINE!*"

"YOU KNOW THAT BIG PICTURE WINDOW THE WILSONS USED TO HAVE?"

"HEY, DID YOU FORGET YOU LEFT ME UPSTAIRS SOAKING?"

"BUT NOBODY'LL SEE ME UNTIL *TOMORROW!*"

"... AN' BLOW WHISTLES AN' HORNS AN' RING BELLS AN' SING SONGS AN' YELL 'HAPPY NEW YEAR'...AND THEN THEY WANTA KNOW HOW COME I'M NOT SLEEPIN'!"

"I HOPE HE TAKES THIS MONEY AND BUYS SOME SEAT CUSHIONS!"

"BEFORE YOU GET MAD . . . . . I WON!"

"I KNOW YOU HATE TO WASH MY CLOTHES WHEN THEY GET DIRTY, SO I THREW 'EM AWAY."

"LOOK AROUND, YOUNG MAN. I'M SUPPOSED TO HAVE ANOTHER BANANA!"

"MAYBE I'D BETTER SEE IF DAD'S GETTING ENOUGH AIR IN THAT CLOSET."

WELL, WE TOOK HIM FOR A CANOE RIDE. ANY MORE BRIGHT IDEAS?

"MY MOTHER ISN'T HOME, BUT I'LL ASK MY DAD IF YOU CAN COME IN. HE'S RIGHT HERE BEHIND THE DOOR."

"SHALL I WRAP THEM, OR WOULD HE LIKE TO SCUFF THEM UP RIGHT AWAY?"

"I'M ALL RIGHT, SO DON'T SNEAK UP ON ME WITH ANY NOSE DROPS!"

"I TRADED THE KITTEN FOR A DOG....THEN I TRADED THE DOG FOR A GOAT...THEN I TRADED THE GOAT FOR..."

"DID YOU KNOW THE PAINT'S COMIN' OFF ONE OF THE LITTLE PIGS THAT STAYED HOME?"

"...YOUR MOTHER *DOES* GIVE US A COUPLE COOKIES, JUST MEMBER THAT DOESN'T MAKE ME YOUR BOY FRIEND OR ANYTHING!"

"MAD, ISN'T SHE?"